NICE FISH

NEW AND SELECTED
PROSE POEMS

NICE FISH

NEW AND SELECTED
PROSE POEMS

BY

Louis Jenkins

HOLY COW! PRESS
DULUTH · MINNESOTA · 1995

ISBN 0-930100-61-1

Publisher's Address: Distributor's Address:
Holy Cow! Press   The Talman Company, Inc.
Post Office Box 3170   131 Spring Street
Mount Royal Station   Suite 201E-N
Duluth, Minnesota 55803   New York, New York 10012

This project was supported, in part, by a grant from the National
Endowment for the Arts in Washington, D.C., from the Arrow-
head Regional Arts Council through an appropriation from the
Minnesota State Legislature, and by generous individuals.

ACKNOWLEDGEMENTS

Some of the poems in this book were published in *An Almost Human Gesture*, The Eighties Press and Ally Press, ©1987 by Louis Jenkins: "Basketball," "Life is so Complex," "A Quiet Place," "The Ukrainian Easter Egg," "First Snow," "Football," "Motorcycle," "War Surplus," "The Ice Fisherman," "The Well-Digger's Wife," "Margaret Luoma," "The Plagiarist," "Twins," "Marlene Nolund," "The Blind Man," "Asleep at the Wheel," "Appointed Rounds," "Sailors," "Frost Flowers," "Intermission," "In a Tavern," "Confessional Poem," "Library," "The Flood," "Violence On Television," "A Photograph," "Invisible," "Walking Through a Wall."

The following poems were published in *All Tangled Up With The Living*, The Nineties Press, ©1991 by Louis Jenkins: "The Lost Boy," "Out-of-the-Body Travel," "A Portrait of the Master," "Mr. Watkins," "Kansas," "The Poet," "Fishing Below the Dam," "Automobile Repair," "A Pool Game," "In the Streets," "Fish Out of Water," "Restaurant Overlooking Lake Superior," "On Aging."

"Sainthood" was published in *Cimarron Review*.

"The Gate" was published in *North Coast Review*.

"Corkscrew," "Spontaneous Combustion," and "Your Baby" were published in *The Prose Poem: An International Journal*.

Thanks to the National Park Service for an Artists' Residency at Isle Royale National Park during which some of these poems were written.

A Few Words About the Prose Poem

It was the freedom of the prose poem which first attracted me, its flexibility which makes it hospitable to images from the unconscious and to conscious narrative, which allows language that is lyrical to coexist with that which is prosaic. I loved the idea of a poem that worked without rhyme, meter or predetermined line breaks, things which insist that the reader should be having a poetic experience. Yet in some ways the prose poem seems to me to be a very formal poem.

The form of the prose poem is the rectangle, one of our most useful geometric shapes. Think of the prose poem as a box, perhaps the lunch box Dad brought home from work at night. What's inside? Some waxed paper, a banana peel, half a peanut butter-jelly sandwich. Not so much, a hint of how the day has gone perhaps, but magic for having made a mysterious journey and returned. The dried out pb&j tastier than anything made fresh.

The prose poem is a formal poem because of its limits. The box is made for travel, quick and light. Think of the prose rectangle as a small suitcase. One must pack carefully, only the essentials, too much and the reader won't get off the ground. Too much and the poem becomes a story, a novel, an essay or worse. We know that a sonnet has fourteen lines but the prose poem is a formal poem with unspecified limits. The trick in writing a prose poem is discovering how much is enough and how much is too much. It's a matter of maintaining balance:

I am welcomed aboard a boat—it's a canoe hollowed from a dark tree. The canoe is incredibly rocky, even when you sit on your heels. A balancing act. If you have the heart on the left side you have to lean a bit to the right, nothing in the pockets, no big arm movements, please, all rhetoric has to be left behind. It's necessary: rhetoric will ruin everything here. The canoe glides over the water.

(from "Standing Up" by Tomas Tranströmer, translated from the Swedish by Robert Bly)

The prose poems in this book were chosen from those I have written over the past twenty-five years. During that time I thought very little about the prose poem form. I simply tried to write as well as I could. Whatever craft I gained, what few ideas I got about form, came from that process. The prose poem is more than the luggage, it is also the journey. Think of the prose poem as a door, another useful rectangle.

THE DELIGHTS OF THE DOOR

Kings don't touch doors.

They don't know this joy: to push affectionately or fiercely before us one of those huge panels we know so well, then to turn back in order to replace it—holding a door in our arms. The pleasure of grabbing one of those tall barriers to a room abdominally, by its porcelain knot; of this swift fighting, body-to-body, when, the forward motion for an instant halted, the eye opens and the whole body adjusts to its new surroundings.

But the body still keeps one friendly hand on the door, holding it open, then decisively pushes the door away, closing itself in—which the click of the powerful but well-oiled spring pleasantly confirms.

(by Francis Ponge, translated from the French by Robert Bly)

Louis Jenkins

TABLE OF CONTENTS

New Poems

They are beyond me, are fishes,
I stand at the pale of my being
And look beyond, and see
Fish, in the outerwards,
As one stands on a bank and looks in.

—from "Fish" by D.H. Lawrence

I

FROM
AN ALMOST HUMAN GESTURE

BASKETBALL

A huge summer afternoon with no sign of rain. . . . Elm trees in the farmyard bend and creak in the wind. The leaves are dry and gray. In the driveway a boy shoots a basketball at a goal above the garage door. Wind makes shooting difficult and time after time he chases the loose ball. He shoots, rebounds, turns, shoots . . . on into the afternoon. In the silence between the gusts of wind the only sounds are the thump of the ball on the ground and the rattle of the bare steel rim of the goal. The gate bangs in the wind, the dog in the yard yawns, stretches and goes back to sleep. A film of dust covers the water in the trough. Great clouds of dust rise from open fields that stretch a thousand miles beyond the horizon.

LIFE IS SO COMPLEX

Life is so complex, even though you eat brown rice and brush your teeth with baking soda. Simplify. Spend the day alone. Spend it fishing. Watch the line and the motion of the water; your thoughts drift . . . a slight bump and a steady pull on the line and the whole line of cars begins to move as the train pulls out of the station. Someone takes the seat beside you, someone at the end of a love affair. The threats of murder and suicide, the pleading, the practical jokes, became at the end only tiresome and she is relieved at his going. She turns away before the train is out of sight.

Your ordinary life is simple, full of promise, bullet-like, pushing aside the waves of air, moving with incredible speed toward the life that waits, motionless, unsuspecting, at the heart of the forest.

A QUIET PLACE

I have come to understand my love for you. I came to you like a man, world-weary, looking for a quiet place. The gas station and grocery store, the church, the abandoned school, a few old houses, the river with its cool shady spots . . . good fishing. How I've longed for a place like this! As soon as I got here I knew I'd found it. Tomorrow the set production and camera crews arrive. We can begin filming on Monday: the story of a man looking for a quiet place.

THE UKRAINIAN EASTER EGG

It is quite different from the ordinary Ukrainian Easter Egg because of the pictures. On one side the sun is setting over Los Angeles and opposite, soldiers sitting in the muddy trenches. They look cold, smoking cigarettes. Here is the violin hidden in the soup kettle and there is a family of cats living in an abandoned gas station. There are so many pictures: the barbed wire and the road through the forest, the ducks, the radio, the yellow, smoky fires along the railroad track where the lovers are taking a walk. In the morning the elders of the village decide what must be done. A brave man must ride the fastest horse and deliver the egg. The journey is long, the roads are dangerous. The egg must be given only to the Czar.

FIRST SNOW

By dusk the snow is already partially melted. There are dark patches where the grass shows through, like islands in the sea seen from an airplane. Which one is home? The one I left as a child? They all seem the same now. What became of my parents? What about all those things I started and never finished? What were they? As we get older we become more alone. The man and his wife share this gift. It is their breakfast: coffee and silence, morning sunlight. They make love or they quarrel. They move through the day, she on the black squares, he on the white. At night they sit by fire, he reading his book, she knitting. The fire is agitated. The wind hoots in the chimney like a child blowing in a bottle, happily.

FOOTBALL

I take the snap from center, fake to the right, fade back . . . I've got protection. I've got a receiver open downfield. . . . What the hell is this? This isn't a football, it's a shoe, a man's brown leather oxford. A cousin to a football maybe, the same skin, but not the same, a thing made for the earth, not the air. I realize that this is a world where anything is possible and I understand, also, that one often has to make do with what one has. I have eaten pancakes, for instance, with that clear corn syrup on them because there was no maple syrup and they weren't very good. Well, anyway, this is different. (My man downfield is waving his arms.) One has certain responsibilities, one has to make choices. This isn't right and I'm not going to throw it.

MOTORCYCLE

He climbs on, switches on the ignition, kicks the starter: once, twice, three, four, five times . . . nothing. He tries a dozen more times. It won't go. He checks the gas tank. Got gas. He switches the key off and on, tries again. It still won't go. He climbs off the bike and squats down to look at the engine. Check the carburetor, check the wires. . . . Seems okay. He takes a wrench from his jacket pocket and removes the spark plug. He examines it, blows on it, wipes it on his jeans, replaces the plug, climbs back on the bike and tries again. Nothing. Now he is getting really angry. There is absolutely no reason why this thing shouldn't start. He gets off the bike and stands and stares at it. He gets back on and kicks the starter really hard half-a-dozen times. Now he is furious. He gets off and throws the wrench he is still holding as far as he can. It bounces on the gravel down the road and skids into the weeds in the ditch. Then he turns and kicks the son-of-a-bitch motorcycle over on its side and walks away. After a short distance he thinks better of it and returns to the motorcycle. It isn't sobbing quietly. It doesn't say "I don't want to play with you any more," or "I don't love you any more," or "I have my own life to live," or "I have the children to think of." It only lies there leaking oil and gas. He rights the motorcycle and carefully wipes off the dust, carefully mounts and once more tries the starter. Even now it won't go. He gets down and sits in the dirt beside the broken motorcycle.

WAR SURPLUS

Aisle after aisle of canvas and khaki, helmets and mess kits, duffle bags, pea coats, gas masks. . . . Somewhere there is a whole field of abandoned aircraft, all kinds, P-38's, B-25's. . . . All you have to do is wait until dark, climb over the fence, pull the blocks from the wheels, climb in, start the engines and taxi out to the strip. It's easy. You can fly without ever having had a lesson.

A beautiful woman dressed in black sits on a bench near a grave. A tall man in dress uniform stands beside her and puts his hand on her shoulder. She says, "I come here often, it is so peaceful." He says, "Before John died, he asked me to look after you." They embrace. Behind them are many neat rows of white crosses extending over a green hill where the flag is flying proudly.

The engines make a deep drone, a comforting sound, and the light from the instrument panel tells you everything is stable and right. Below are silver-tufted clouds and tiny enemy towns, lovely toy towns, all lighted by the bomber's moon.

THE ICE FISHERMAN

From here he appears as a black spot, one of the shadows that today has found it necessary to assume solid form, and along with the black jut of shoreline far to the left, is the only break in the undifferentiated gray of ice and overcast sky. Here is a man going jiggidy-jig-jig in a black hole. Depth and the current are of only incidental interest to him. He's after something big, something down there that is pure need, something that, had it the wherewithal, would swallow him whole. Right now nothing is happening. The fisherman stands and straightens, back to the wind. He stays out on the ice all day.

THE WELL-DIGGER'S WIFE

I've been thinking of mountains on these hot nights, or better yet, the window ledge high above the bed and this tangle of sheets. It must be cool there with the breeze from the open window, and clean, painted white, like snow, only not so cold or wet. And not so steep as a mountain top, like a great plain stretching out for miles. I started to move there once, last summer, taking just a few things I'd need: the cat, the mirror, a hatful of needles. But then he came home and caught me, broke two of my ribs and put an ugly bruise on my cheek. Every day now the sound of digging grows more faint. The sound of boots slogging through the mud is gone and the rocks roll away miles below me.

MARGARET LUOMA

At her age a fall could have meant a serious injury, a sprained ankle or a broken hip. Luckily there was only a bruise and the terrible embarrassment. She pulled away from the young man who helped her to her feet, said "Thank you, I'm all right" and went on her way as quickly as she could without looking back. But she couldn't forget about it. His face . . . like a photograph on the piano, thoughtful, always young. "All that concern," she thought. "What did he care?" It began to seem as though he'd caused the bruises, actually pushed her down. She didn't need him. She was old now. A lifetime of love wasted.

THE PLAGIARIST

A fat teaching assistant has caught a freshman cheating on his exam and she stands now in the hallway displaying the evidence, telling the story to her colleagues: "I could tell by the way he looked. I could tell by his hands." With each detail the story expands, rooms are added, hallways, chandeliers, flights of stairs, and she sinks exhausted against a railing. More listeners arrive and she begins again. She seems thinner now, lighter. She rises, turns. She seems almost to be dancing. She clutches the paper of the wretched student. He holds her firmly, gently as they turn and turn across the marble floor. The lords and ladies fall back to watch as they move toward the balcony and the summer night. Below in the courtyard soldiers assemble, their brass and steel shining in the moonlight.

TWINS

The first baby they brought into my room was a girl. I held her for a few minutes then the nurse took her away. I never saw the baby again or the nurse that brought her. Later another nurse brought the boy, my son. When I told my husband he said it was probably just the effect of the anesthetic, but I made him check. They said there was only one baby born, a boy. I'm certain now there were two. I know the little girl is alive somewhere but I have no idea how to find her. I can only watch her brother for signs . . . you know, the way twins sense things about each other. Sometimes I'm afraid when he goes off to school, lost among so many other children. When he comes home in the afternoon I catch him and hold him a moment and look into his eyes before he pulls away to run outside and play with his friends. I can't really say what I'm looking for. I think I'll only know if something is missing, a certain look or a gesture. . . . I think I'll know if that life dies out in him. I can't explain that to him, of course, or to his father, he would only say I've got too much imagination.

MARLENE NORLUND

She's packed the kids off to spend the weekend with their father. At last she has the place to herself, a rented farmhouse, a couple dozen chickens, a pickup that works part-time and a child support check she finally managed to get from her ex-husband. His problem was that he didn't want anything much. He was happy being a bricklayer or being in the army, happy just hanging around the house. She puts on her best dress and stands in front of the mirror brushing her hair. She looks good, a little big in the chest maybe, but good for being the mother of two. It's midafternoon and the whole weekend is ahead. The summer wind nags at the house and flaps the blind at the window behind her so that it sounds like someone impatiently turning the pages of a newspaper. She imagines a man there, lying on the bed, glancing up occasionally to hurry her along, jingling the change in his pocket. It makes her nervous and angry. She fidgets with the dress, extracts a pair of earrings from the clutter of perfume and baby bottles on the bureau, smears her makeup. She hurries. It isn't what she wants.

THE BLIND MAN

He comes down the hill at a slight angle to the sidewalk, hesitantly, moving his red-tipped white cane from side to side until it touches the fender of a lavender Pontiac parked at the curb. Then he stops. He reaches out with his left hand until he touches the cold metal pole of a No Parking sign, pulls himself close, stands with his arm wrapped around the pole in the narrow space between pole and car, waits and listens. He seems unsure, seems to have difficulty sorting the various sounds. Traffic to the right, traffic behind, wind blowing uphill from the Lake, the sound of a few leaves on the concrete. No passersby. End of the day, end of fall. He listens, head slightly raised, hat pushed back, eyes closed. He is neither young nor old; a man between a car and a pole. He waits a long time. Then he moves his cane to the right, up into the rear wheelwell of the car, then away to the left. He releases the pole and takes two careful steps downhill, moving the cane in front of him.

ASLEEP AT THE WHEEL

He falls asleep at the wheel and dreams that everything is the same. He is still driving at night through the big pine forest. Mile after mile glides through the automobile. He manages distances more easily now so there is time to discern in the night forest a single tree, a stone, or a hidden path. These things seem as familiar and absorbing as a love affair or his own childhood. He sees for the first time that the forest extends not fifty or a hundred miles, but infinitely on either side of the road, and that it is possible to wander there forever, alone, and not die. . . . The car veers into the gravel at the edge of the blacktop. He wrenches the wheel back to the left. He is wide awake. The car is on the road, speeding toward the end of its headlight beams.

APPOINTED ROUNDS

At first he refused to deliver junk mail because it was stupid, all those deodorant ads, money-making ideas and contests. Then he began to doubt the importance of the other mail he carried. He began to randomly select first class mail for non-delivery. After he had finished his mail route each day he would return home with his handful of letters and put them in the attic. He didn't open them and never even looked at them again. It was as if he were an agent of Fate, capricious and blind. In the several years before he was caught, friends vanished, marriages failed, business deals fell through. Toward the end he became more and more bold, deleting houses, then whole blocks from his route. He began to feel he'd been born in the wrong era. If only he could have been a Pony Express rider galloping into some prairie town with an empty bag, or the runner from Marathon collapsing in the streets of Athens, gasping, "No news."

SAILORS

When the ship gets into port the sailors all go nuts. They get drunk and dance and wake up the next afternoon in the whorehouse. And if a sailor gets thrown in jail he doesn't care because he just got paid and has enough money to get out. None of the sailors wants to go back to the ship. One thing sailors can't stand is the sight of water. One sailor hides out in a laundromat. One makes plans to marry. Another is still drunk. The sailors hate this lousy port. The ship sails at dawn with all hands, but someone has sneaked whiskey aboard. By midnight the crew is drunk and the ship is dead in the water. The captain is furious and shouts over the intercom to the engine room. But they are all asleep, rocked in their little cradle on the sea.

FROST FLOWERS

In the morning people go off to work all wrapped and bundled, through frozen doors, over cracking snow, huffing and puffing, each fueled by some simmering private indignation: low pay, something that was said at coffee break. . . . The sun is far away on the southern horizon, a vague hope, more distant than the Caribbean. Eight below zero at eleven o'clock. The coffee boils and grows bitter. All afternoon the same old thing, knucklebone of mastodon, stews on the stove. The radiator hisses at the long shadows which finally engulf the winter day. Lights come on for a time in the houses and go out one by one. We breathe deeply of the dark, we exhale great plumes and fronds that form on the windows, intricate icy blossoms open around us all night.

INTERMISSION

The violins have gone, the brass and woodwinds have gone. The orchestra has just finished a Paganini concerto. The basses and cellos lie on the floor or recline against chairs, weary and unimpressed. They are like soldiers or prisoners on a ten minute break and no one has any cigarettes. In a far corner, dressed in black, the percussionist hunches over the tympany like a raven picking over a rabbit killed on the highway or like an old woman bending over a kettle brewing a poison to be painted on telephone poles to kill all the woodpeckers. He tunes and tests the drum. What does he hear? A distant storm? A herd of buffalo? Perhaps railroad crews working hard to lay down track a few miles ahead of a locomotive; the cars richly furnished with carpet, crystal and fine wine. The beautiful ladies and gentlemen come laughing and talking down the aisles to find their seats.

In a Tavern

"It's no use," he says, "she's left me." This is after several drinks. It's as if he had said, "Van Gogh is my favorite painter." It's a dimestore print he has added to his collection. He's been waiting all evening to show it to me. He doesn't see it. To him it's an incredible landscape, empty, a desert. "My life is empty." He likes the simplicity. "My life is empty. She won't come back." It is a landmark, like the blue mountains in the distance that never change. The crust of sand gives way with each step, tiny lizards skitter out of the way. . . . Even after walking all day there is no change in the horizon. "We're lost," he says. "No," I say, "let's go on." He says, "You go on. Take my canteen. You've got a reason to live." "No," I say, "we're in this together and we'll both make it out of here."

CONFESSIONAL POEM

I have this large tattoo on my chest. It is like a dream I have while I am awake. I see it in the mirror as I shave and brush my teeth, or when I change my shirt or make love. What can I do? I can't remember where I got the tattoo. When in the past did I live such a life? And the price of having such a large tattoo removed must be completely beyond reason. Still, the workmanship of the drawing is excellent, a landscape 8 x 10 inches in full color, showing cattle going downhill into a small western town. A young man, who might have been my great-grandfather, dressed as a cowboy and holding a rifle, stands at the top of the hill and points down toward the town. The caption beneath the picture reads: "Gosh, I didn't know we were this far west."

LIBRARY

I sit down at a table and open a book of poems and move slowly into the shadow of tall trees. They are white pines, I think. The ground is covered with soft brown needles and there are signs that animals have come here silently and vanished before I could catch sight of them. But here the trail edges into a cedar swamp: wet ground, dead fall and rotting leaves. I move carefully but rapidly, pleased with myself. Someone else comes and sits down at the table, a serious looking young man with a large stack of books. He takes a book from the top of the stack and opens it. The book is called *How to Get a High-Paying Job*. He flips through it and lays it down and picks up another and pages through it quickly. It is titled *Moving Ahead*. We are moving ahead more rapidly now, through a second growth of popple and birch, our faces scratched and our clothes torn by the underbrush. We are moving even faster, marking the trail, followed closely by bulldozers and crews from the paper company.

THE FLOOD

Every so often, a girl calls me on the phone and tells me that she loves me, can't live without me, etc. The first time she called I was intrigued and flattered, naturally. But when I asked her name she ignored me and went right on talking. "Could we meet somewhere?" Again she ignored the question. Finally I became irritated and hung up. Obviously it was some kind of joke. She called several more times over the next few months and each time the result was the same. "What's the point?" I ask. "I love you," she says. A few weeks ago the bridge on 21st Street washed out. People came from all over town to help with the work and to watch the river overflow its banks and pour through the streets, the first flood in many years. Men were hard at work piling up sandbags to hold back the water. Near where I was standing, a pay telephone kept ringing and ringing. Finally, since no one else did, I answered. I thought perhaps it was someone calling with instructions for the flood control workers, but no. It was a man having trouble with his refrigerator. I guess he thought I was a repairman. No sooner had he hung up than the phone rang again; a woman looking for her child. No, I hadn't seen him. Call after call came in. It was as if people were actually telephoning the flood. For some reason I kept answering the phone. Then she called. "Hello," a pause. "Hello," I said again. "Louis," she said, "Louis—is that you?" I hung up the phone and stepped out of the booth. It was a relief to be in the open air again. I stood a moment looking at the muddy water while the phone continued to ring.

Violence on Television

It is best to turn on the set only after all the stations have gone off the air and just watch the snowfall. This is the other life you have been promising yourself; somewhere back in the woods, ten miles from the nearest town, and that just a wide place in the road with a tavern and a gas station. When you drive home, after midnight, half drunk, the roads are treacherous. And your wife is home alone, worried, looking anxiously out at the snow. This snow has been falling steadily for days, so steadily the snow plows can't keep up. So you drive slowly, peering down the road. And there! Did you see it? Just at the edge of your headlight beams, something, a large animal, or a man, crossed the road. Stop. There he is among the birches, a tall man wearing a white suit. No, it isn't a man. Whatever it is it motions to you, an almost human gesture, then retreats farther into the woods. He stops and motions again. The snow is piling up all around the car. Are you coming?

A Photograph

She's been dead fifty years now. This photo was taken in 1902, just a girl, clowning for the camera. But when a baby is born in the family someone says, "See it has her eyes, her nose." And it's true. The argument continues. "I'm a farmer," I say, "a business man. I can't be wasting time in town, hanging out at the cafe, drinking coffee." It's spring and the roads are impassable. I stand in the barnyard, knee deep in mud, dumbfounded, surrounded by insolent chickens. She says, "I never want to leave here." At night she whispers, "You have never loved me. You think only of yourself. You won't be allowed to enter the promised land." Then she giggles and pokes me in the ribs. "The children are asleep now," she says.

INVISIBLE

There are moments when a person cannot be seen by the human eye. I'm sure you've noticed this. You might be walking down the street or sitting in a chair when someone you know very well, your mother or your best friend, walks past without seeing you. Later they'll say, "Oh, I must have been preoccupied." Not so. At times we are caught in a warp of space or time and, for a moment, vanish. This phenomenon occurs often among children and old people. No one understands exactly how this happens but some people remain invisible for long periods of time. Most of these do so by choice. They have learned to ride the moment, as a surfer rides the long curl of a wave. How exhilarating it is to ride like that, a feeling of triumph to move from room to room unseen, only the slightest breeze from your passing.

WALKING THROUGH A WALL

Unlike flying or astral projection, walking through walls is a totally earth-related craft, but a lot more interesting than pot making or driftwood lamps. I got started at a picnic up in Bowstring in the northern part of the state. A fellow walked through a brick wall right there in the park. I said, "Say, I want to try that." Stone walls are best, then brick and wood. Wooden walls with fiberglass insulation and steel doors aren't so good. They won't hurt you. If your wall walking is done properly, both you and the wall are left intact. It is just that they aren't pleasant somehow. The worst things are wire fences, maybe it's the molecular structure of the alloy or just the amount of give in a fence, I don't know, but I've torn my jacket and lost my hat in a lot of fences. The best approach to a wall is, first, two hands placed flat against the surface; it's a matter of concentration and just the right pressure. You will feel the dry, cool inner wall with your fingers, then there is a moment of total darkness before you step through on the other side.

II

FROM
ALL TANGLED UP WITH THE LIVING

THE LOST BOY

When Jason did not come home from school on the bus Barbara began to worry. She went next door to ask if Bobby, who rode the same bus, had seen Jason. Bobby remembered seeing Jason but didn't think he got on the bus. Bobby's mother, Teresa, said, "Oh, he probably just decided to walk." Teresa thought Barbara was a silly woman who fussed over her children. Bobby and Chris set out to look for Jason. It was an adventure, a search through the dark continent. Barbara used Teresa's phone to call the school. Meanwhile, Jason returned home, went in the back door and up to his room. Through the open window he could hear his mother in the next yard. He flopped down on the bed and looked at comics. He could hear his mother talking about calling the police. He lay looking at the big crack in the ceiling. He thought about what it was like to be lost. He thought he could hear voices, far away, calling his name.

OUT-OF-THE-BODY TRAVEL

Body and soul are linked as in a marriage, a sort of three-legged race team, and are usually comfortable with this arrangement. If the soul is forced to travel alone it does not wing its way over wide water, does not fly skimming the tree-tops. No, the soul shuffles along like any body, eating at lunch counters, listening to conversation in the bus station restroom. . . "Fifty cents? I think I can get fifty cents . . . ," riding the bus all through the dark night, watching the distant, singular lights go past, wondering all the while if this trip was really necessary. Meanwhile the body sits, inert, staring at the t.v., needing a shave, a nail trim.

A Portrait of the Master

In this picture Jesus stands, surrounded by followers, with his right arm partially raised, his index finger, slightly crooked, pointing upward. His left arm extends downward, palm open. He looks as he often does in pictures, white robe, sandals, beard neatly trimmed. His hair is rather long but clean. His face is calm, unwearied, because Jesus maintains, even thrives under the pressure of constant travel and the demands of those who flock to him. These are a ragged bunch, malcontents, the disenfranchised, those for whom heaven is impossible, the only ones who show any interest at all in what he has to say. They want help, they come to tell their stories, to ask questions, but mainly to listen. They have the sense that He is one of them, only better. And though the word He brings is difficult, it is the saying that is important. We must continually explain ourselves to ourselves. There is no one else to listen. He says again: "Here is the earth. Here is the sky."

MR. WATKINS

When Mr. Watkins discovered one of the old gods dead in the crawl space under the house he put on his overalls, tied a bandanna over his nose and mouth and worked his way beneath the low cobweb covered floor joists on his belly. He planned to drag it out by the heels but as soon as he touched the corpse there was a flash and a pop like a downed powerline. Mr. Watkins' heart stopped and the air smelled of ozone. The resulting fire completely destroyed the house and the garage.

Stray dogs, squirrels, flights of harpies roosting on the t.v. antenna, angels and devils only too ready to spirit you away. . . .

At night Mr. Watkins used to patrol his 75 x 150 foot lot with a flashlight. You could hear his cough, see the light bobbing over the damp grass in summer, over the snowbanks in winter. Mr. Watkins was an old man and forgot things easily but he knew where the property lines were drawn and, by god, if you don't know that you don't know anything.

KANSAS

As she smells the clean sheets the farmer's wife thinks of the 1930's. Wind whips the clothes on the line, blows her dress tight against her heavy legs.

The farmer in his dirty overalls searches through years of broken machinery behind the barn, searches through tall sunflowers, through the nests of rabbits and mice with a wrench in his hand, looking for exactly the right part or one that might do.

Seven skinny cows lie in the mud where the tank overflows. Throughout the long afternoon the windmill continues to pump long draughts of cool water.

THE POET

He is young and thin with dark hair and a deep, serious voice. He sips his coffee and says "I have found that it is a good idea to check the words you use in a dictionary. I keep a list. Here is the word *meadow*. Since I was a child the word *meadow* always had connotations of peace and beauty. Once I used *meadow* in a poem and as a matter of practice I looked the word up. I found that a *meadow* was a small piece of grassland used to graze animals. . . . Somehow *meadow* was no longer a thing of beauty. . . . "

It is spring. A few cows are grazing in the muddy meadow. There are patches of blackened snow beside the road. It is nearly dark and the ragged poplars at the far end of the meadow have turned black. The animals, the stones, the grass, everything near the earth darkens, and above: the *azure sky*.

FISHING BELOW THE DAM

On summer evenings the working men gather to fish in the swift water below the dam. They sit on the rocks and are silent for the most part, looking into the water and casting again and again. Lines tangle, tackle is lost and a fisherman curses to himself. No one notices. It is simply a part of the routine, like the backs of their wives in bed at night or short words to the children in the morning. Only the water holds their attention, crashing through the spillway with enough force behind it to break a man's back. And the undertow that could take you as easily as a bit of fishline and toss you ashore miles downstream. The men shout to be heard above the roar of the water. *ANY LUCK? NO I JUST GOT HERE.*

AUTOMOBILE REPAIR

It's raining and the car stalls with Mama, the kids and a full load of laundry inside. At least the warning lights still work. You raise the hood and find yourself staring, once again, into the void. Fuel pump? Alternator? The trick is to keep this thing running without spending any money, akin to making something from nothing. Thus Jehovah, confronted with a similar difficulty, simply began assembling the salvaged parts of the previous universe. Once you have located the problem you're ready (two or three cups of coffee will help) to plunge into the mud and grease. This time it's easy. The wire from the coil to the distributor has fallen off. It's running again—bald tires, broken exhaust, rust. . . .

A POOL GAME

They share a cuestick. He breaks, makes the four ball and misses a shot on the six. He puts the cue down carefully, an archbishop surrendering the symbols of the church. He offers a few words of advice on her first shot. She picks up the cue as if it were the Olympic torch and starts off around the table. She puts away the nine, fifteen and the eleven. Bam. Bam. Bam. And this is for you. Pow! The ten. He sits at the bar, bored. He's been playing for so many years. She thinks the game has possibilities, just needs a little work, a little fixing up. She misses a shot on the twelve. He gets up slowly. She is trying to lug a large cement statue of St. Francis into the backyard by herself. He goes to help. Secretly though, it makes him mad. He'll have to fight through the Pacific from island to island again. He's such an old soldier. He picks up his weapon and goes after the deuce and the tray.

IN THE STREETS

He carries everything he owns in a paper bag. What are you? A broken alarm clock? A returnable pop bottle? Once, on this very corner, a man hit him in the mouth. That's why some of his teeth are missing. It was drink made that man hit him. He never drinks. He waits for you everyday with his hand out. Everyday without fail. It's a wonder he's still alive. The coldest days he spends at the public library. But where does he go at night? The moon is shining now at four in the afternoon and down here it's all wind and shadows. In the streets with the blowing snow and newspapers he carries on the same argument with his parents, though they have been dead thirty years. At the mouths of alleys he pauses. . . . He is an only child. All he wants is his share.

FISH OUT OF WATER

When he finally landed the fish it seemed so strange, so unlike other fishes he'd caught, so much bigger, more silvery, more important, that he half expected it to talk, to grant his wishes if he returned it to the water. But the fish said nothing, made no pleas, gave no promises. His fishing partner said, "Nice fish. You ought to have it mounted." Other people who saw it said the same thing, "Nice fish. . . ." So he took it to the taxidermy shop but when it came back it didn't look quite the same. Still, it was an impressive trophy. Mounted on a big board the way it was, it was too big to fit in the car. In those days he could fit everything he owned into the back of his Volkswagen but the fish changed all that. After he married, a year or so later, nothing would fit in the car. He got a bigger car. Then a new job, children. . . . The fish moved with them from house to house, state to state. All that moving around took its toll on the fish, it began to look worn, a fin was broken off. It went into the attic of the new house. Just before the divorce became final, when he was moving to an apartment, his wife said "Take your goddamn fish." He hung the fish on the wall before he'd unpacked anything else. The fish seemed huge, too big for this little apartment. Boy, it was big. He couldn't imagine he'd ever caught a fish that big.

RESTAURANT OVERLOOKING LAKE SUPERIOR

Late afternoon. Only a few old men at the bar, drinking and talking quietly. Waitresses for the evening shift begin to arrive. One stands for a moment at the far end of the dining room and looks out the window facing the lake. Snow is falling. The lake is completely obscured, still customers will ask for tables near the window. A few early diners begin to arrive, then others. Soon the room is filled with sounds—people talking, the rattle of dishes, the waitresses hurrying about. The lake is a great silence beneath all the noise. In their hurry the waitresses don't look out the window. Yet they are in her service, silent a moment as they fill the glasses with water.

ON AGING

There are no compensations for growing old. Certainly not wisdom. And one gave up anticipating heaven long ago. Perhaps there is a kind of anesthesia resulting from short-term memory loss, from diminished libido, from apathy and fatigue which is mistaken for patience.

The rich can afford to grow old gracefully but the flesh of the poor shows each defeat like a photographic plate that records the movement of the planets and the stars and the rotation of the earth. Eyesight fails and hearing, the skin wrinkles and cracks, the bones twist, the muscles degenerate. . . . It takes all morning to open a can of soup.

The world collapses inward. Memory is no recompense. The past is fiction, a story of interest only to the young. There is only, as there always was, the moment. The instant, which, when you become aware of it, is blinding as the flash when someone snaps a picture of you blowing out the candles.

III

NEW POEMS

CORKSCREW

The woman next door comes over to return a corkscrew.
"Thanks for letting us use this. I'm sorry you couldn't make it
to the party." I don't remember being invited to a party. I just
stand at the door with the thing in my hand as she goes. I look
at it dumbly and don't recognize it. This isn't *my* corkscrew.
Well, I don't really own this corkscrew or anything else, for
that matter. That has become more apparent to me as time
goes by. This is just another thing that came to my door of its
own volition, out of some instinctual urge perhaps, the way
bees swarm into a tree, piling up, forming what seems to be a
single living shape; or came by accident, the way the wind
makes a dust devil out of dirt and straw, whatever is at hand.
It careens across the field, picks up a newspaper, picks up a
driver's license, picks up a college degree . . . . "Margaret, I'd
like you to meet Louis. He's not the guy I was telling you
about." "Really? Who are you then?"

NOVEMBER

I don't love the woods it occurs to me, the leafless, brushy, November popple trees that stand around, stand around crowding the peripheral vision, each waiting to take its place in my consciousness and each falling back to become a part of the line that divides gray earth from gray sky, as undistinguished as gray hair.

Over there one shaft of sunlight penetrates the clouds as if it were an indicator. As if something was being called to my attention. What? More frozen trees? What is it? It's as if someone leaving on a train says something as the cars begin to move, something through the glass. I can see his lips moving. Gestures. What? I can't hear you. What?

INSECTS

Insects never worry about where they are. A mosquito is so dedicated to the pursuit of warm blood that it neglects the long range plan. If a mosquito follows you into the house it waits patiently until the lights are out and you are nearly asleep then it heads straight for your ear. Suppose you miss, hit yourself in the head and knock yourself out and the mosquito succeeds in drawing blood. How will it get out of the house again to breed? What are its chances?

Insects don't seem to have a sense of place but require only a certain ambiance. A fly that gets driven 500 miles in a car and then is finally chased out the window does not miss the town where it spent its maggothood. Wherever this is it will be the same; a pile of dog shit, a tuna salad sandwich, a corpse.

The Language of Crows

A crow has discovered a scrap of roadkill on the blacktop and can't resist telling everyone in a loud voice. Immediately another crow arrives on the scene and the fight begins, cawing, flapping, and biting. Suddenly crows come flying in from every direction to enter the battle, skimming low over the treetops, all cawing loudly. Finally one crow (it's impossible to tell which) makes off with the prize and flies a few hundred feet into the trees. But as soon as he stops the others are on him and the melee begins again. This scene is repeated time after time and each time the crows move farther away into the woods until their cawing has grown faint but remains undiminished in intensity. Crows have a limited vocabulary, like someone who swears constantly, and communication seems to be a matter of emphasis and volume.

If you lie quietly in bed in the very early morning, in the half-light before time begins, and listen carefully, the language of crows is easy to understand. "Here I am." That's really all there is to say and we say it again and again.

Spontaneous Combustion

As the late afternoon sunlight comes in through the window, one thing then another, a chair, a photograph, a glass on the table, is illuminated then fades as the sun moves on. It is as if a thought became suddenly conscious, a few words of an old song perhaps, "gaudeamus igitur something something . . . " something you never understood but that remained with you anyway. It is that time when one is, finally, no longer a child but not yet old, full of strength and light, a time that passes so quickly, never to return. But then, who knows? After all it wasn't the young lovers ignited by passion, though there were rumors. . . . It was just an old man, no permanent address, a sister living in Toledo. An old man wearing everything he owned, two old coats, worn trousers, three shirts, wool long johns and a hat. Perhaps it was the old clothes like oily rags and the irritation of wool on skin that set the spark. Some irritation, some annoyance. His soul rose above the flames like the ashy skeleton of a piece of newspaper still glittering at the edges, then broke apart, disappeared in the brisk March wind.

The Night Room

There is one bedroom in the east wing where it is always night. It is a favorite with the overworked rich and famous as a place to catch up on some much needed rest. Elizabeth Taylor spends a week of every year in the night room and Ed McMahon (or is it Dick Clark?) often comes here to vacation. The room is on the ground floor and has access to a private walled garden which was added in the 16th century after the unusual properties of the room were discovered. If you open the curtains you can see the moonlight reflected on the water in the little fountain or the stars shining above the garden wall even though it may be noon on a sunny day. It would be curious to see into the room from the garden, if that were possible, to watch the room's current occupant, perhaps reading by lamplight or asleep, a shadowy form on the bed, unaware that it is now nearly three in the afternoon. And if awakened he or she would, no doubt, see you the same way, as a shadowy form between the hibiscus and the lemon verbena, possibly dangerous.

DRIP

Water does not want to be still. The ocean rages in its bed even though there is nowhere to go. Down, always down. When a fissure opens in the ground water pours in. On to the center of the earth!

Water has come to a halt here in the swamp. Stymied. All life here eventually ends up as muck under the water. You can reach down and bring up a hundred years in a single handful; the substance of things hoped for.

Water does not want to be contained. Silently, secretly, water feels along the walls of the pipe for a flaw, seeks the misthreaded joint, the faulty faucet. . . . The drips go orderly, joyfully into the sink counting the seconds of the long night.

WINTER LIGHT

The distant January sun glitters at a low angle through the bare trees making a pattern of stripes, varied widths of sunlight and shadow, across the road. The car moves along like a scanner over a bar code. This is the tally of a very protracted shopping trip. Light and dark, light and dark. . . . It's the old duality: good and evil, male and female, dogs and cats, etc. The strobe light flashes of sun are hypnotic, dangerous, creating the illusion that the car is stopped and that the road is no more than a series of still photographs projected on a screen . . . or the opposite—that you've been somewhere, that you are on your way somewhere.

AFTER SCHOOL

She had made a kind of promise to herself not to stop, but his house was right on her way home, besides, she thought, it was OK because they were just friends, they had always been just friends. . . . But, of course, he wasn't home when she knocked and his mother seemed like she was in a bad mood or something, but then his mother often seemed that way. . . . When she looked up again it was nearly dark. Lights were on in the houses. The last sunlight shone red and orange on the bare birch trees and on the snowdrifts. It was beautiful, perfectly still, almost like a painting, she thought. And she was the one in the picture, walking home after school, always, toward supper and the long winter night.

YOUR BABY

Cry and curse, stamp your foot down hard, because the surface of the earth is no more than a crust, a bunch of loose tectonic plates, something like the bones of a baby's skull, floating on a core of molten magma: chaos and anarchy, the fires of hell. And as you've been told repeatedly, it's all in your hands. It's like the egg you were given in Marriage and Family class. "This is your baby, take care of it." So dutifully you drew a smile face on, then as an afterthought added a pair of eyebrows shaped like rooftops. It gave the egg baby a slightly sinister appearance. Then a friend added Dracula fangs and said, "See it looks just like its daddy." "Let me see" someone said and another gave your elbow a shove.

Late at night. Where is your demon child now, as you sit dozing over the periodic tables?

THE GATE

The gate makes a few hesitant moves in the wind, allowing some dry leaves to blow into the yard. Then as if suddenly determined to leave forever, the gate swings wide open, bounces off a snowbank and slams shut. It remains still for a time, as if stunned by the experience. Then it begins again, moving a few tentative inches before the big rush. The gate is teased by the wind. It can only break at the hinges. It's useless. The gate is set in its ways.

WEST WIND

Trees fling themselves about in order to evict the noisy birds. A little boy leans into the wind and runs. He wants to fly with the crows. He flaps his arms and squawks. Mother is determined, runs after, grabs him and straps him into the stroller seat. "You stay right here." The little boy wants to fly like the wrapper from a hamburger, all brightly colored, into the busy sky.

So many plans, but the stakes are broken, the string knotted and tangled. Yet one is filled with a sense of accomplishment. For a moment I hold the car keys in my hand and for some time afterwards feel I have just returned from a long trip.

How to Tell a Wolf from a Dog

A wolf carries his head down, tail down. He has a look of preoccupation, or worry, you might think. He has a family to support. He probably has a couple of broken ribs from trying to bring down a moose. He's not getting workman's comp, either, and no praise for his efforts. The wolf looks unemployed, flat broke.

On the other hand, a dog of similar features, a husky or a malamute, has his head up, ears up, looks attentive, self-confident, cheerful and obedient. He is fully employed with an eye toward promotion. He carries his tail high, like a banner. He's part of a big organization and has the title of "man's best friend."

ANGELS

Contrary to popular belief angels have no important function in the array of mythic beings. They seem to be primarily decorative, hovering above a saint pierced with arrows or part of a heavenly chorus, white and shining in the sky. They are like yachts skimming the blue, so beautiful in the sun. Useless as guardians or messengers, they have a lot of time on their hands. One has lingered too long among humans, fascinated by the possibility of a toothache or unrequited love. Heedless that his wings will no longer lift him more than a foot or so off the ground, one shuffles down the street at dusk, pretending to be a nineteenth-century poet, a misunderstood genius, hunched over in his great cape.

FREEWAY

Just south of Pine City a car passes me from behind. I glance over at the driver. It's my old girlfriend from 25 years ago! Exactly the same, she hasn't aged a day. The same blond, wind-blown and frazzled hair, the same intent look. She's on her way back to Texas probably, all her stuff loaded inside. She's on her way to get some money out of her ex, or to some other desperate appointment that will finally make the difference. . . . Whatever I'm into now, whatever I've become, she doesn't want to know. She won't look at me. She knows you can't take your eyes off the road for even an instant.

CAMPSITE

He paddles the canoe across the still water, alone in the evening, back to his camp. The water is perfect for walking, flat as the floor of a ballroom. This evening only the shadows of spruce walk out from the forest, a time of darkening reflection. He pulls the canoe onto the shore and turns it over in just the way that his ancestors did. He builds a fire the way they did except that he uses matches. He does not speak. His ancestors did not speak. They could only grunt and point. He does not know who his ancestors were except that they, like him, were notorious liars. He sits in a circle of light. An owl calls out from the trees. He sits in the smoke and pokes at the glowing coals with a stick. He moves a little to the left. The smoke follows him. He moves a little to the right.

SAINTHOOD

Because of my extraordinary correctness and sensitivity of late I have been elevated to the status of Temporary Minor Saint (secular). The position comes with a commendation praising my "uncharacteristic reticence tantamount to sagacity." This means that my entire being is now suffused with a pale radiance somewhat like the light from a small fluorescent bulb, the light on a kitchen range perhaps, only not quite so bright, and that instead of walking I now float at an altitude of approximately three inches above the ground. I move about at a slow and stately speed as befits my new rank. I move to the left or right by inclining my head and upper body in the appropriate direction. It's a less-than-perfect condition. The light keeps my wife awake at night and though the added height is beneficial, moving about in a crowd presents difficulties. My forward speed seems to be fixed and, though slow, is quite tricky to stop. I lean back but momentum carries me forward like a boat. Suddenly turning my head can send me veering into the person next to me or into a wall. In order to remain in one place I've found it necessary to attach cords to my belt on one end and to various solid objects around the room on the other. These days I take my meals standing up, tethered like the *Hindenburg*.

THE VIEW FROM SCOVILL POINT

This is not the end, but you can see the end from here. Well, often when you think you have come to the end there is one more thing. Out there is a scattering of islands some of them thick with spruce and balsam, marshes and bogs. Easy to get bogged down with last minute details. It's better to think of each island as a stepping stone. Flag Island, South Government, North Government, Merritt Island, and last of all Passage Island with its light, not the light at the end of the tunnel, not the warm encompassing light, just a brief flash and then . . . it comes again. Beyond all are the open waters of Lake Superior. . . . Each passenger receives a hug, a bouquet of flowers, a small box of candy.

SNOW HOLLOWS

That's where he sleeps, that ne'er-do-well half-brother of yours, in the snow hollow, that patch of dry ground on the south side of the big spruce tree, where the branches hang down, heavy with snow, a place protected from the wind and weather. Somewhat. In a few days he'll move to another place much like this one. Each time one of those trees bends down to touch his head a little more gray appears in his hair. Well, what did he expect? He thinks the world owes him a living. Now and then the winds blow his way—bringing a page of yesterday's newspaper. He's out there now in the blue after-noon gloom with his great expectations, his moose call and that ridiculous hunting knife with its fringed leather scabbard. Let him stay out there.

The Cure for Warts

Draw a circle in red around the wart while repeating the incantation, words not to be spoken aloud in the presence of another human being. Once those words are spoken to someone else they are forever changed and you must begin again. A few words to say in the silence and the dark. A phrase to worry over, polish and perfect, to believe in, despite all evidence to the contrary. In a few weeks the wart should drop off. But magic is so approximate. Perhaps only a wheel cover comes loose from your car as you drive down the interstate and rolls into the ditch. No chance of retrieving it in the heavy traffic. Later perhaps one of the ubiquitous crows spots it there in the high grass and flies down to admire his reflection in the shiny surface. Beautiful. Fascinating. He opens his beak to sing. Yes, perhaps he'll sing.

THE MIND READER

He says, "The mind leaps the way a salmon flashes in the air. So quick you think you might have imagined it. The mind leaps to protect its darkest secret thus giving it away. But that is of no interest to me. What I need to know is the date of birth or the number of keys on the key ring."

Tonight the mind reader has retired early with a blond woman he met at the show, the one with the "interesting mind." On the bedside table with the watch and wallet is his hidden communication device. If you put the tiny earpiece to your ear you can hear a faint sound, like the sound of the sea, the distant hiss and crackle of the autonomic nervous system.

NO HIRED MAN

It turns out that everything I've written is untrue. It wasn't entirely innocent. For instance, when I described a woman kneeling down near the creek, I knew that it wasn't a woman but a pile of brush, a few rags and some shreds of polyvinyl. Worse. When I think about it now I realize that there was no brush pile. No creek, either.

One evening after supper, when I was three or four years old, the hired man said "I'll make you something." He took a couple of brazing rods from the welder and spent a long time twisting them together with pliers. I tried to wait patiently. Then suddenly he said "It won't work" and threw the thing on the pile of scrap metal outside the garage. After he had gone, walking the long road into town, I looked at the thing he'd made. I carried it around for awhile then put it back on the scrap heap. I never found out what he intended to make. Or what it was.

Louis Jenkins' poetry has been published in a number of magazines and anthologies including *American Poetry Review, Gettysburg Review, Kenyon Review, Poetry East, Paris Review* and *Virginia Quarterly Review*. His books of poetry include *An Almost Human Gesture* (Eighties Press and Ally Press, 1987) and *All Tangled Up With The Living* (The Nineties Press, 1991). Mr. Jenkins has twice been awarded the Bush Foundation Fellowship for Poetry and was a winner of the Loft-McKnight Award for Poetry in 1987. He lives with his wife and son in Duluth, Minnesota.